BASEBALL LEGENDS

Hank Aaron
Grover Cleveland Alexander
Ernie Banks
Johnny Bench
Yogi Berra
Roy Campanella
Roberto Clemente
Ty Cobb
Dizzy Dean
Joe DiMaggio
Bob Feller
Jimmie Foxx
Lou Gehrig
Bob Gibson
Rogers Hornsby
Reggie Jackson
Shoeless Joe Jackson
Walter Johnson
Sandy Koufax
Mickey Mantle
Christy Mathewson
Willie Mays
Stan Musial
Satchel Paige
Brooks Robinson
Frank Robinson
Jackie Robinson
Pete Rose
Babe Ruth
Nolan Ryan
Mike Schmidt
Tom Seaver
Duke Snider
Warren Spahn
Willie Stargell
Casey Stengel
Honus Wagner
Ted Williams
Carl Yastrzemski
Cy Young

NEWFIELD
PUBLICATIONS

BASEBALL LEGENDS

REGGIE JACKSON

Norman L. Macht

Introduction by
Jim Murray

Senior Consultant
Earl Weaver

CHELSEA HOUSE PUBLISHERS
New York • Philadelphia

Published by arrangement with
Chelsea House Publishers.
Newfield Publications is a federally
registered trademark of Newfield
Publications, Inc.

CHELSEA HOUSE PUBLISHERS

Editorial Director: Richard Rennert
Executive Managing Editor: Karyn Gullen Browne
Copy Chief: Robin James
Picture Editor: Adrian G. Allen
Art Director: Robert Mitchell
Manufacturing Director: Gerald Levine

Baseball Legends
Senior Editor: Philip Koslow

Staff for REGGIE JACKSON
Copy Editor: Catherine Iannone
Editorial Assistant: Kelsey Goss
Designer: M. Cambraia Magalhães
Picture Researcher: Alan Gottlieb
Cover Illustration: Daniel O'Leary

Library of Congress Cataloging-in-Publication Data

Macht, Norman L. (Norman Lee), 1929
Reggie Jackson / Norman L. Macht; introduction by Jim Murray;
senior consultant, Earl Weaver.
    p. cm. (Baseball legends)
ISBN 0–7910–2169–6
1. Jackson, Reggie Juvenile literature. 2. Baseball
players United States Biography Juvenile literature.
[1. Jackson, Reggie. 2. Baseball players. 3. Afro-
Americans   Biography.] I. Title. II. Series.
GV865.J32M33 1994   94–228
796.357'092 dc20   CIP
[B]   AC

CONTENTS

WHAT MAKES A STAR 6
Jim Murray

CHAPTER 1
MR. OCTOBER 9

CHAPTER 2
BLACK IN A WHITE TOWN 15

CHAPTER 3
GETTING TOUGH 21

CHAPTER 4
"FANS DON'T BOO NOBODIES" 27

CHAPTER 5
"THE STRAW THAT STIRS
THE DRINK" 35

CHAPTER 6
SWEET AND SOUR 41

CHAPTER 7
THE LAST DINGER 49

CHRONOLOGY 59
STATISTICS 61
FURTHER READING 62
INDEX 63

WHAT MAKES A STAR

Jim Murray

No one has ever been able to explain to me the mysterious alchemy that makes one man a .350 hitter and another player, more or less identical in physical makeup, hard put to hit .200. You look at an Al Kaline, who played with the Detroit Tigers from 1953 to 1974. He was pale, stringy, almost poetic-looking. He always seemed to be struggling against a bad case of mononucleosis. But with a bat in his hands, he was King Kong. During his career, he hit 399 home runs, rapped out 3,007 hits, and compiled a .297 batting average.

Form isn't the reason. The first time anybody saw Roberto Clemente step into the batter's box for the Pittsburgh Pirates, the best guess was that Clemente would be back in Double A ball in a week. He had one foot in the bucket and held his bat at an awkward angle—he looked as though he couldn't hit an outside pitch. A lot of other ballplayers may have had a better-looking stance. Yet they never led the National League in hitting in four different years, the way Clemente did.

Not every ballplayer is born with the ability to hit a curveball. Nor is exceptional hand-eye coordination the key to heavy hitting. Big-league locker rooms are filled with players who have all the attributes, save one: discipline. Every baseball man can tell you a story about a pitcher who throws a ball faster than anyone has ever seen but who has no control on or *off* the field.

The Hall of Fame is full of people who transformed themselves into great ballplayers by working at the sport, by studying the game, and making sacrifices. They're overachievers—and winners. If you want to find them, just watch the World Series. Or simply read about New York Yankee great Lou Gehrig; Ted Williams, "the Splendid Splinter" of the Boston Red Sox; or the Dodgers' strikeout king Sandy Koufax.

A pitcher *should* be able to win a lot of ballgames with a 98-miles-per-hour fastball. But what about the pitcher who wins 20 games a year with a fastball so slow that you can catch it with your teeth? Bob Feller of the Cleveland Indians got into the Hall of Fame with a blazing fastball that glowed in the dark. National League star Grover Cleveland Alexander got there with a pitch that took considerably longer to reach the plate; but when it did arrive, the pitch was exactly where Alexander wanted it to be—and the last place the batter expected it to be.

There are probably more players with exceptional ability who didn't make it to the major leagues than there are who did. A number of great hitters, bored with fielding practice, had to be dropped from their team because their home-run production didn't make up for their lapses in the field. And then there are players like Brooks Robinson of the Baltimore Orioles, who made himself into a human vacuum cleaner at third base because he knew that working hard to become an expert fielder would win him a job in the big leagues.

A star is not something that flashes through the sky. That's a comet. Or a meteor. A star is something you can steer ships by. It stays in place and gives off a steady glow; it is fixed, permanent. A star works at being a star.

And that's how you tell a star in baseball. He shows up night after night and takes pride in how brightly he shines. He's Willie Mays running so hard his hat keeps falling off; Ty Cobb sliding to stretch a single into a double; Lou Gehrig, after being fooled in his first two at-bats, belting the next pitch off the light tower because he's taken the time to study the pitcher. Stars never take themselves for granted. That's why they're stars.

1

MR. OCTOBER

Jackson crushes a Burt Hooton delivery for a two-run homer during the fourth inning of Game 7 of the 1977 World Series. Known as Mr. October for his post-season heroics, Jackson was at his best in pressure-packed situations: appearing in 27 World Series games, he batted .357, with 10 home runs and 24 RBIs.

Reggie Jackson was in a groove as he drove his blue Volkswagen through New York traffic to Yankee Stadium on the afternoon of October 18, 1977. The Yankees led the Los Angeles Dodgers, 3 games to 2, in the World Series, largely because of Jackson's power hitting. He had hit a home run and a double in the New Yorkers' 4–2 win in Game 4, and even though his team had lost Game 5, Jackson had hit a home run off Don Sutton in his last time at bat. Sutton had tried to take advantage of Jackson's supposed weakness as a hitter by pitching him up and in, but Jackson had crushed the ball anyhow.

Jackson was still pumped up when he went out to take batting practice at 6:40. The bat felt light and quick in his hands. Usually, Jackson was the last Yankee to take his practice swings when the other team was waiting their turn in the batting cage. He could put on an intimidating show for the opposition and the early-bird fans, driving pitch after pitch into the farthest reaches of the ballpark. If there was one thing Reggie Jackson craved more than hitting dingers (as he called home runs), it was having an audience to admire them.

The Dodgers seemed unfazed by the pregame show as they took a 2–0 lead in the top of the first. When Jackson led off the second, Dodgers pitcher Burt Hooton walked him on four pitches, none of them close enough to swing at. Chris Chambliss followed with a home run to tie the score.

In the fourth, Jackson came up to bat with a man on first, aching for a ball close enough to hit. He got one, lofting the first pitch into the seats to give the Yankees a 4–3 lead.

Elias Sosa was pitching for Los Angeles when Jackson came up in the fifth with Willie Randolph on first. He prayed for a strike he could get his bat on, and his prayer was answered. "He tried to come inside," Jackson said, "and I hit that one better than the first. As I was running down the line I was yelling, 'Stay up, stay up' and it did."

Jackson's blast put the Yankees ahead, 7–3. By the time Jackson came up again in the eighth inning, the crowd was frenzied with anticipation. Charlie Hough, who threw nothing but knuckle-balls, was on the mound for the Dodgers. Jackson had a knack for timing a knuckler, which can drive hitters crazy with its unpre-dictable fluttering. The names of knuckleball pitchers he had touched for dingers flashed through his mind as he strode confidently to the plate. Always aware of his audience, Jackson knew that, even if he struck out, he would get a standing ovation from the crowd.

On the mound, Hough said to himself, Don't walk him, whatever you do. He did not want the boos of the throng cascading down on him. As the first pitch fluttered toward the plate, it looked like a beach ball to Jackson. He could not wait for it to come within range. He swung and hammered the longest drive of the night,

deep into the center-field bleachers. "It was a pretty good pitch," Hough later recalled, "around the knees, and he killed it. I put him into the Hall of Fame."

Jackson felt as if he were floating around the bases. As he passed first base, even Dodgers first baseman Steve Garvey secretly applauded in his glove. The howling din did not let up until Jackson came out for a curtain call. Only Babe Ruth had hit 3 home runs in a World Series game, but not even the Babe had blasted 3 in a row. Jackson stood alone among the great World Series sluggers.

Jackson gets a hero's welcome in the Yankees dugout after belting his third consecutive home run in Game 7 of the 1977 Series, leading the Yankees to their first world championship in 15 years.

There was still the top of the ninth to be played, but the crowd could not have cared less. They had one thing on their minds: swarming onto the field to get to Jackson when the last out was made. The fans in right field began hurling firecrackers, and Jackson wore his batting helmet while playing his position. Bottles and cherry bombs rained down on the occupants of the Dodgers bullpen.

When the final out came on a pop-up to the pitcher, Jackson dashed through the descending mob like the running back he had been in high school. "It was pandemonium, total chaos," recalled Willie Randolph. "All you could hear was the deafening sound of people. It's a little scary, having all those people going nuts running on the field. But it was one of the most exciting moments I've ever witnessed."

Jackson considered those three home runs— four in a row, counting the one he had hit in his last at-bat the night before—the most important he had ever hit. In addition to the personal glory they brought him, they won the World Series for his team, and despite his ego, which was immense, Jackson was above all a team player.

For the public, Jackson's World Series heroics, earning him the nickname Mr. October, sum up his 21-year career. Baseball insiders, who often have a different slant on the game, remember him for other feats. Hall of Famers Frank Robinson and Jim Palmer remember Jackson most of all for his awesome blast in the 1971 All-Star Game, played in Detroit's Tiger Stadium. The ball was still rising when it hit a transformer on a rooftop light tower. Palmer, who was warming up in the bullpen, recalled, "I heard the bat and looked around—there was silence. Everyone was watching the ball. You just don't see balls hit like that."

Kansas City superstar George Brett, one of the game's finest all-around hitters, may have paid Jackson the ultimate compliment: "If you were in the dugout and you knew Jackson was due to hit, you didn't go to the bathroom, even if you had to. You waited."

Many players and fans disliked Jackson. There was no denying that he had a big ego and a big mouth. He was accused of being arrogant and acting like a hot dog. "There isn't enough mustard in the world to cover that guy," a teammate once commented. But whether people loved him or hated him, they never took their eyes off him. And that was all Reggie Jackson ever asked for.

2

BLACK IN A WHITE TOWN

Reginald Martinez Jackson was born on May 16, 1946, in Wyncote, Pennsylvania, a predominantly white suburb of Philadelphia. His parents, Martinez and Clara, belonged to Wyncote's small black community. (Martinez Jackson's mother had been Spanish, accounting for his somewhat unusual first name.) Young Reggie joined a large household that included a brother named James and a sister named Beverly, in addition to a half brother, Clarence, and a half sister, Dolores, both from his father's earlier marriage. Another sister, Tina, arrived a few years later. They all lived above Martinez Jackson's tailor shop on a busy street that featured two gas stations and the Wyncote Market.

Martinez Jackson's store was in the white business district; most of his customers were the white professionals and businessmen who commuted between the suburbs and their jobs in the city. This put Reggie in a quandary as he grew up: he was accepted and liked by the white storekeepers on the block, but he was turned away by the all-white boy scout troop and barred from the houses of his white friends. Later he could recall only two families whose doors were open to him; one was the family of a

Jackson as he appeared in his 1964 high school yearbook. Growing up black and poor in a mostly white suburb, Jackson experienced a need for approval and affection that he carried into adulthood—he also developed a sense of pride and a determination to succeed as an athlete.

school friend, Michael Frankel, the other of a girl he had a crush on, Jill Connors. "The parents of my best friend, George Beck, did not allow us to play together," he said. "We had to sneak off. We didn't understand it, but that's the way it was." When Reggie was six, his parents separated. One day his mother was there and the next day she was gone, to Baltimore, taking Beverly, James, and Tina with her. Jackson was left with Dolores and Clarence, both much older than he, and his father.

Martinez Jackson struggled to provide for his family. On cold winter days, the only heat in the apartment came from the kitchen oven. There was food on the table for every meal, but nothing extra in the cupboard or refrigerator. Reggie never had a hot breakfast. Cleanliness ranked as the highest priority. Reggie carefully swapped his school clothes for play clothes after school every day. His socks did not always match, but they were always clean.

Reggie ran errands in the neighborhood for his father. He once stole a candy bar while he and his father were shopping in the Wyncote Market. When his father saw Reggie eating the candy, he marched his son back into the store and made him confess to the store owner. The only thing Reggie ever stole after that was 233 bases.

Martinez Jackson knew what it was like to be treated as a second-class citizen. He told Reggie about the great players in the Negro leagues— Satchel Paige, Josh Gibson, and others—who could not play in the big leagues because of the color of their skin. But Jackson was not consumed by bitterness or anger. He told his son, "Don't whine and don't complain. Go out and do your job and earn the money they're paying you." He impressed on Reggie the importance of speaking clearly, using proper English in order to be listened to with respect. Although the elder Jackson worked long hours every day, he found time to play ball with Reggie. He had been a semipro player in his youth, but an injury he received while serving in the air force during World War II left him with a slight limp that made him look as if he were strutting when he walked. He encouraged Reggie to play all sports in school. "But if you don't make the first-string teams," he said, "you have to come home after school and do chores around the house and help in the store."

Reggie played Little League and Babe Ruth League baseball. At 13 he was only 5 feet 4 inches tall and weighed 98 pounds, but he made the junior varsity football team as a quarterback. "I had a girlfriend taller than I was," he recalled. "But I would play any position to make the first-string team and get out of doing chores around the house."

There was one part of the cleaning business that Reggie enjoyed: the deliveries. Riding in the Ford panel truck with Greenwood Avenue Cleaners painted on the side started his lifelong passion for cars. The Jacksons' yard was usually home to five or six junkers at a time, and Reggie became an expert mechanic by working to get them running. Later, his father helped him buy a 1955 Chevy, which remained his favorite even after he collected many more exotic and expensive cars.

Reggie began rooting for the Philadelphia Athletics, but when the team moved to Kansas City, he switched his allegiance to the Phillies.

Jackson (44) closes in on a punt returner during a 1964 high school game. Though he also excelled at baseball, basketball, and track, Jackson preferred football because it gave him the opportunity to let out his anger and frustration.

He admired Jackie Robinson of the Brooklyn Dodgers for breaking the color line in baseball. He also idolized some of the other black stars who followed Robinson into the major leagues, especially Willie Mays, Hank Aaron, and Bob Gibson. Gibson, he said, "showed me competitiveness just by the way he took the mound. I developed my approach to playing from watching him."

As a teenager, Reggie absorbed the powerful influence of two very different black leaders, and their impact never left him. Heavyweight champion Muhammad Ali inspired pride, confidence, and bravado in him. "At that time many black people were embarrassed by being colored, straightening their hair. Ali spoke to us: be proud of your heritage and yourself," Jackson later said. "As a minority, you grope for some identity, and he was a positive one for us." From the Reverend Martin Luther King, Jr., Jackson learned that pride could be expressed with eloquence and style as well as with fists or a football or a baseball bat.

One afternoon in the fall of 1963, the 17-year-old Jackson came home and found two police cars parked outside. The police had come to arrest his father for making illegal corn whiskey in the basement of the store and for taking part in a numbers operation. With his father in jail for six months, Reggie was left alone to go to classes, play four sports after school, and keep the tailor shop open. His brother, James, came back to help him run the business and provide him with some money and clothes.

Reggie excelled as a running back and basketball player, ran the 100-yard dash in 9.6 seconds, and pitched three no-hitters for the baseball team while batting .370. College football recruiters and big league baseball scouts followed his achievements with great interest, but there were no parents at home for them to talk to. Reggie's own preference was for football. "I was a stiff-backed, awkward baseball player, too muscular and crude," he said. "But football came more natural to me—no need to control your temper, you didn't need patience, you could vent your venom."

He accepted a football scholarship from Arizona State University (ASU). In August 1964, with $50 in his pocket, he got into ASU football star Gene Foster's 1956 Pontiac and took off for Tempe, Arizona, about as far from 149 Greenwood Avenue in Wyncote as he could get.

3

GETTING TOUGH

When he arrived at Arizona State, Jackson, like many young athletes, fell from being a high school headliner to just another freshman among all-stars from all over the country. He was intimidated by the sight of a gigantic lineman whose body filled the hallway in the dorm.

ASU football coach Frank Kush, who never smiled, believed in bruising, punishing workouts. He would give the ball to Jackson and order him to run a play into the defensive line—with no blocking in front of him. It was like running head-on into five hostile redwood trees with arms. "Can't take it, Jackson?" Kush would bark. "Not tough enough? Try it again."

Then there was The Mountain: day after day the players had to run up a steep incline covered with rocks, trees, and cacti, dodging scorpions and snakes in the 100-degree-plus desert heat. Jackson survived and made the freshman team, but as a defensive back.

Jackson had no intention of playing baseball at ASU. But one day in the spring of 1965, after football practice, two friends bet him five dollars he could not make the baseball team. Five dollars went a long way for Jackson in those days, and besides, playing baseball would get him out of the brutal spring football drills. So, still in his

Jackson swings the bat as a member of the Arizona State baseball squad. Though he attended ASU on a football scholarship, Jackson went out for the baseball team on a bet and quickly established himself as a fleet-footed, power-hitting phenomenon.

football uniform, he walked over to the diamond where coach Bobby Winkles watched his players practice. Winkles had a national reputation for developing big league players. That summer, slugger Rick Monday would sign with the pros for $100,000; infielder Sal Bando had gone to the majors earlier.

Jackson took off his helmet and shoulder pads, picked up a bat, and asked if he could take a few swings. Given a nod, he rocketed 14 balls over the fences in all directions and collected the five-spot.

Jackson wanted to spend the summer of 1965 with his mother in Baltimore, and he also wanted to gain some baseball experience. Coach Winkles called Walter Youse, manager of Leone's, one of the top amateur teams in the country, and asked him to give Jackson a try-out.

"We were working out at Swann Park near the Baltimore harbor one day when Jackson drove up in this little Pontiac Le Mans," Youse recalled. "He introduced himself and I put him up to bat and he hit 400-foot drives one after the other halfway to the harbor where nobody else had ever hit them. Then I said, 'Let me see you bunt and run to first,' and held a stopwatch on him. He flew down the line in 3.3 seconds. I thought there must be something wrong with the watch. The fastest anybody had ever been timed was Mickey Mantle and Richie Ashburn at 3.1. So I asked him to do it again. He did it again in 3.3. I asked him to throw from the out-field to home and he threw bullets. He had the best tools I ever saw: power, speed and arm strength. He was never a good hitter, but he had the power."

Youse took Jackson to Memorial Stadium so that Baltimore Orioles manager Hank Bauer could take a look at him. After Jackson launched several balls into orbit, Bauer wanted to sign him, but the player draft had started the year before and the rules prevented teams from signing players before their sophomore year.

Jackson's sophomore football season at ASU frustrated and upset him. He rebelled at playing safety, even as the defensive captain. Running backs got the headlines while defensive backs got the bruises, and Jackson wanted to be the center of attention. He was also hassled for dating white women, and he resented the taunts and barbs aimed at him.

In the spring of 1966, Jackson discovered that baseball could be fun. The Sun Devils won 41 and lost 11. Jackson hit .327 with 15 home runs and 65 RBIs in the short college season, and he fell in love with whacking dingers as thousands stood and cheered him. He was still a crude, awkward

Jackson and Kansas City Athletics vice-president Ed Lopat meet with reporters in June 1966, after Jackson signed with the Athletics for an $85,000 bonus. With the help of Gary Walker, a college classmate and close friend, Jackson later parlayed his baseball earnings into lucrative real estate ventures.

outfielder, in need of instruction and discipline. Coach Winkles worked with him, stressing hustle on every play. He chewed out Jackson for failing to run out a pop fly. "Kush made me tough," Jackson said, "and Winkles taught me the discipline needed to play baseball." Rick Monday's signing for $100,000 had opened Jackson's eyes. His father was barely earning a living. Although he still preferred football, he was now eligible for the major league draft. When the Kansas City Athletics made him the number two choice in the 1966 draft, Jackson asked for a $100,000 bonus.

He had no idea what that much money looked like. Anything more than $10 was a lot of money to him. But the figure had a nice ring to it, and Walter Youse had told him he was worth as much as Monday.

Athletics owner Charlie Finley flew Jackson and his father to Chicago, then took them in a private plane to his Indiana farm. There he offered $50,000. Jackson said no. Finley raised it to $75,000. Jackson called Coach Winkles, who advised him to take the money and ask for two years' college expenses, too. At the last minute Jackson took a deep breath and asked Finley to throw in a new Pontiac. Finley agreed.

Jackson began the 1967 season in the minors, in Birmingham, Alabama. But the Athletics were going nowhere and drawing few fans. So Finley called up Jackson and catcher Dave Duncan to create some news and excitement. Wearing number 9, Jackson made his big league debut on June 9, 1967. His first hit was a triple off Orlando Peña of the Indians, but he struck out frequently. Despite a backpack full of confidence and big talk, he was scared and overwhelmed. After three weeks, the Athletics sent him back to Birmingham, where he brooded over his failure to shine from day one. Recalled to the big club in September, Jackson hit his first big league home run on September 17 at Anaheim, California.

At the Kansas City spring training camp in 1968, all the minor leaguers and rookies were crowded into the back of the clubhouse for meetings. Jackson told another rookie, Rene Lachemann, who was sitting beside him, "This is the last year I'm sitting back here."

And it was.

4

"FANS DON'T BOO NOBODIES"

Jackson began the 1968 season on the bench in Oakland, California, where the A's had moved from Kansas City. One day, manager Bob Kennedy pointed to right field and told Jackson, "You have a chance to take over that position." Jackson replied, "That guy out there is just subbing until I get ready."

When he did take over right field, he hit 29 home runs, but he also led the league with a near-record 171 strikeouts while batting only .250. He broke quite a few bats on the water-cooler or dugout steps in frustration after striking out.

The A's had finished last during their final year in Kansas City, and nobody cared about them in the eastern or national media. This lack of interest was a break for Jackson. "I had skills but was crude," he said, "and I could play in obscurity until I could mature and grow and improve." That obscurity disappeared forever in 1969.

Jackson started the 1969 season hitting home runs at a pace that left Babe Ruth, Roger Maris, and all the other great home run hitters in the dust. He looked as if he might hit 100. One day in June, he drove in 10 runs in Boston. On July 2, he hit 3 home runs in one game.

Jackson confers with Washington Senators slugger Frank Howard prior to the 1969 All-Star Game. At the time, Jackson was leading the majors with 37 home runs and threatening to break Roger Maris's single-season record of 61; though he fell well short with 47, his home run tear made him a national celebrity.

The first indication that Jackson stepped it up a notch whenever the national television cameras were on him came on a Saturday afternoon against the Minnesota Twins, at the old Metropolitan Stadium in Minneapolis. The game was being broadcast throughout the country as the Game of the Week; with the nation's baseball fans watching, Jackson hit the longest dinger of his career off pitcher Jim Perry. The ball hit 60 feet up on the center-field scoreboard, 521 feet from home plate. Had the scoreboard not been in the way, Jackson's blast might have soared 600 feet.

By the first week of August, Jackson had 41 home runs, well ahead of Maris's record 61-homer pace of 1961. Now the media were watching every move he made. At 23, Jackson had become an instant superstar. But he soon discovered that the bright light of celebrity could burn. He quickly tired of answering the same old questions every day and finding a microphone stuck in his face every time he turned around.

Too immature to handle the sudden flood of fame, Jackson went homer happy on every pitch the rest of the season. Manager Hank Bauer tried to get him to bunt more often to take advantage of his speed. "Mickey Mantle used to add 12 points a year to his batting average by drag bunting," Bauer told him. But Jackson refused. Twelve points on his batting average meant nothing to him. "If I hit the ball on the nose the fielders won't catch it," he insisted and swung for the fences. But he hit just 6 more home runs to finish with 47, not even enough to lead the American League. Although he led in strikeouts for the second of four straight years, fanning no longer upset him. The fans had begun to ooh and aah with admiration of his mighty swings whether he connected or just stirred the air. He was not the least bit disturbed when the crowd razzed him after a strikeout. "Fans don't boo nobodies" became his motto.

Jackson had earned $20,000 for his big year. He felt entitled to big money the following spring and asked for $60,000. Charlie Finley said no, and Jackson had to hold out through spring training in order to wring $50,000 out of the owner. During the negotiations, Finley tried to tear down Jackson's performance, emphasizing his strikeouts. Reading the negative comments about himself in the newspapers trampled Jackson's ego and pride, which were the most vital elements of his personality.

He rode the bench during the early season. Finley played mind games with him, grinding his pride in the dirt by asking him to go down to the minors. Frustrated and miserable, Jackson made fielding errors and mental mistakes, got fined, squabbled with the manager and other players, and tried to dodge reporters and fans. It was all contrary to his nature, which was to go all out on every play, every swing, and to invite attention. The game became a job he had to go to every day to collect his paycheck.

He batted just .237 and hit 23 home runs, and none of them gave him any joy. Doubt began to mar his confidence. "Maybe the pitchers have found me out," he lamented. He considered quitting. The world might not have heard any more of Jackson if not for two men who made a winner out of him: Frank Robinson and Dick Williams.

Charles O. Finley, owner of the Kansas City Athletics and then Oakland A's, shows his flair for publicity during a 1965 visit to New York. A self-made millionaire and a shrewd judge of baseball talent, Finley was also a domineering boss who harassed his managers and squabbled over money with his star players.

Following the disastrous 1970 season, Charlie Finley sent Jackson to Puerto Rico to play for Frank Robinson in the Winter League. Robinson had been a hard-nosed, aggressive player, and Finley asked him to work Jackson hard and force him to grow up.

Jackson was down on himself; for the first month he batted about .190, and his dingers were few and far between. The more Robinson chewed him out, urging him to bear down and get tough, the more he dogged it. One day Jackson hit an infield pop-up and failed to run it out. Robinson blew his cork. "If that happens again," he yelled, "you're coming out of the game."

A few innings later, Jackson hit another pop-up and again quit running halfway to first. "See you later," Robinson snarled.

"I'm going home," Jackson said.

Robinson snapped, "Wait till the end of the inning and I'll help you pack."

The manager followed Jackson into the clubhouse, determined not to let the pouting player give up on himself. "Do you want to play baseball or not?" he demanded. "If you're going to play this game, do it at the best level you are capable of. Be the best you can be."

Angry and hurt, Jackson sought out teammate Elrod Hendricks, a catcher for the world champion Baltimore Orioles. "I don't have to take all this abuse," Jackson moaned. "I can go back to school, and I have plenty of outside business interests."

The two men sent out for hamburgers. "He was talking and crying the whole time," Hendricks recalled. "But it really just made him more determined than ever, and he did rise to the challenge. I was leading the league at the time with about 10 home runs and he had maybe 3, but he went on a tear and passed me like I was standing still."

The arrival of Dick Williams as manager in 1971 brought the budding A's into full bloom. They won the American League West for the next four years and took three straight World Series between 1972 and 1974. Williams, a hard-driving leader who got more out of his players than they knew they had in them, had previously taken charge of the Boston Red Sox, a ninth-place team in 1966, and had led them to a pennant in 1967. "Williams was death on mental mistakes," recalled catcher Mike Hegan. "He was up at the top step of the dugout to let you know when you made one. He required that you execute, and if you didn't, you were going to be in trouble with him."

Jackson later acknowledged that Williams had taught him how to win and how to give himself up for the sake of the team. Before that happened, the two men went through turbulent times. Once, Jackson hit a ball he thought would go out of the park, and he started to go into his home run trot. But the ball hit the top of the fence, and he barely made it safely to second base. Afterward he told Williams, "That'll never happen again." And it never did.

The championship years contained almost as much frustration as glory for Jackson. He fought over money with Finley every spring, reaching a salary of $80,000 in 1973. In 1971, when the A's lost to Baltimore in the American League playoff, Jackson lay on the dugout steps and cried with disappointment. In the 1972 playoff against Detroit, he tore up his leg sliding

Jackson connects during the 1972 American League playoff against the Detroit Tigers. A knee injury during the final game of the playoffs knocked him out of the World Series, but Jackson came back with an MVP season in 1973, leading the A's to their second straight world championship.

home on the front end of a double steal and had to sit out the World Series against the Cincinnati Reds, which the A's won without him.

But Jackson put it all together in 1973, batting .293 and leading the league with 32 homers and 117 RBIs. In the World Series, he beat Tom Seaver and the Mets single-handedly in Game 6 and hit his first Series home run in Oakland's 5–2 seventh-game victory. The baseball writers unanimously named him the league's most valuable player; he was only the sixth player in 52 years to top every ballot.

Most pitchers and managers came to regard Jackson as the one man they did not want to see at the plate in the late innings with the game on the line. While many players talk about wanting to bat in those situations, nobody ever doubted that Jackson genuinely, fervently desired the do-or-die swings. "If he was promised he could be in that situation every night, he would pay to get into the ballpark," commented Hal McRae of the Kansas City Royals.

Many players described him as having a giant ego; others called it arrogance. But according to Elrod Hendricks, "What the world saw as arrogance was the clumsy, heavy-handed efforts of a shy, lonely man reaching out for love and attention."

Whenever Jackson played in Baltimore, he asked public address announcer Rex Barney to wait until it was quiet before announcing him as the batter, so he could hear all the boos. "Fifty thousand people could be booing him and he loved it," Barney said. "Cheers or boos, it all meant he was at the center of attention. It psyched him up; it was a challenge to produce, to crank it up a notch. He would even egg on the booing fans and get everybody worked up, including himself. He told me it would really hurt if he went up to bat and there was no crowd reaction at all."

For the rest of Jackson's career, that would never be a problem.

5

"THE STRAW THAT STIRS THE DRINK"

*Montreal Expos man-
ager Dick Williams
gives Jackson a tour
of Montreal's Olympic
Stadium in November
1976. The Expos
vigorously pursued
Jackson as a free
agent during the off-
season; but despite
his high regard for
Williams, Jackson
decided to sign with
the New York
Yankees.*

Coming off his triumphant 1973 season, Jackson believed he was the best player in baseball, and he expected to be paid accordingly. The following spring, major league baseball introduced salary arbitration. A player could state the salary he wanted; the team owner countered with the amount he was willing to pay. The two sides then met before an arbitrator. The player made his case by comparing his statistics with those of other players who were earning the money he was asking for, while the owner brought up the player's weaknesses. Preparing his case, Jackson asked other MVP winners what they had earned after winning the award; he settled on $135,000. Finley offered $100,000. Jackson won.

Jackson led all players in the fans' voting for the 1974 All-Star team, and the A's won their third straight world championship, steamrollering the Dodgers in five games. Confidently, Jackson went to arbitration again in the spring of 1975, asking for $165,000. This time he lost, and the trashing he took at the hearings crushed his ego. "I had a tough time adjusting after losing," he told a reporter. "I was unhappy and it was a burden going to camp." Although he led the league with 36 home runs and the A's won the division title again, the Red Sox swept Oakland in the playoffs. For a team that had aspirations of matching the great baseball dynasties of the past, watching the World Series on television was a dismal experience. Led by Jackson, the A's spent the 1975 season clamoring for more money from the tightfisted Finley. Trying to keep his players in line, Finley did the unthinkable. On April 2, 1976, he traded Jackson and pitcher Ken Holtzman to Baltimore for Don Baylor, Mike Torrez, and Paul Mitchell. "Being traded was a shock," Jackson later wrote. "I was hurt, embarrassed.... It woke me up that I was not too big to be traded. I cried on leaving my friends and home. It was the most traumatic thing I ever went through in my career."

Jackson held out for $200,000, reported late, and missed the first few weeks of the season. The Orioles finished second to the Yankees; most of the players believed they could have won if Jackson had been there from the start, and he agreed.

Free agency came into effect following the 1976 season, and it was clear that the Orioles would not pay Jackson as much as he could command elsewhere. The Padres, Expos, White Sox, and Phillies pursued him, but there was never any real doubt that Jackson was headed for New York, the biggest stage of all. When he signed a five-year, $2.9 million contract on November 29, the press conference resembled a royal coronation; the team captain, catcher Thurman Munson, placed a Yankees cap on Jackson's head as cameras whirred and clicked and politicians applauded. It was the last untroubled day Jackson had in New York.

The Yankees had won the pennant the year before but had been swept in the World Series by the Cincinnati Reds. They were a team of cliques, small groups of players who stuck together and excluded other players. Jackson instantly became the highest-paid member of the team. Munson resented this, and his closest pals shared his anger.

The animosity in the clubhouse smoldered until Jackson ignited it with his own mouth. He gave a lengthy interview to a magazine writer; the more he talked, the more he impressed himself with the sound of his own words. Finally, he said, "I'm the straw that stirs the drink [in New York]. Munson thinks he can be the straw...but he can only stir it bad."

When the story appeared in May, Jackson immediately regretted his brash words. But it was too late. His fate was sealed. He was left with only one friend on the Yankees, backup catcher Fran Healy. "I was the most disliked guy in the clubhouse," Jackson said, "and Healy saw a human in need."

"What did I do for Jackson?" Healy reflected.

Jackson coaxes a smile out of Yankees catcher Thurman Munson during a dinner honoring Munson in February 1979. Despite Jackson's consistent performance on the field, he was never accepted by Yankees veterans such as Munson, who resented his high salary and oversize ego.

"I listened and when he asked my opinion, I gave it to him, good or bad. I never held back." On a team where nobody, including manager Billy Martin, liked him, Jackson clung to the one person he could count on for honest, straight opinions and advice, and he never forgot Healy's kindness to him.

As the season progressed, the Yankees began to resemble a three-ring circus. To the delight of the media, players squabbled with Martin and Yankees owner George Steinbrenner; Martin and Steinbrenner sniped at each other; and Jackson shook hands with nobody after hitting a home run.

After a June 18 confrontation with Martin that nearly ended in a fistfight right in the dugout, on national televsion, Jackson complained to reporters, "It makes me cry the way they treat me on this team.... I'm a big black man with an IQ of 160 making $700,000 a year, and they treat me like dirt. They've never had anyone like me on their team before." In truth, the Yankees were not used to anyone like Jackson. They were a quiet, proud team with a

During his years with the Oakland A's, Jackson once remarked, "If I played in New York, they'd name a candy bar after me." Following his home run barrage in the 1977 World Series, a New York candy manufacturer made Jackson's quip a reality.

Chocolaty covered caramel and peanuts

long tradition of winning. Martin and Munson were longtime favorites in New York, where Jackson was seen as the bad guy, the odd man out. The fans booed him loud and often, but that never dismayed Jackson. In order to boo him, they had to buy tickets, and Jackson filled seats like nobody else in the game. His long-ball hitting and showmanship mesmerized a new generation of young fans.

After a slow start, the Yankees took over first place on August 24 and won the A.L. East by 2½ games over Baltimore. After going 1-for-14 in the first 4 games of the playoff against Kansas City, a dismayed Jackson sat on the bench as lefty Paul Splittorff, a pitcher who had always given him fits, started the deciding game for the Royals. But with New York down 3–1 in the eighth, he drove in a run with a pinch-hit single, and the Yankees went on to win the deciding game on a Chris Chambliss home run, 5–3.

In the World Series against the Dodgers, Jackson was quiet while the Yankees won 2 of the first 3 games, but from then on it was the Reggie Jackson show. Hours after his record-breaking fifth home run capped the Yankees' Series victory and the last celebrant had left the clubhouse, Jackson was still in uniform, savoring the biggest night of his career. When he finally dressed and left at one o'clock in the morning, he left alone.

He drove to his favorite New York restaurant, Jim McMullen's, and celebrated the world championship with a group of friends. Hugh Carey, the governor of New York, later joined them at Jackson's invitation. "We stayed there until five o'clock in the morning," Jackson recalled. "I left right from there to go do the 'Today Show.' That was my night."

SWEET AND SOUR

Yankees manager Billy Martin and Reggie Jackson never got along. Martin seemed unable to appreciate Jackson's efforts on the field, and he resented the star's close off-the-field relationship with team owner George Steinbrenner.

On July 17, 1978, in Kansas City, the friction between the two men ignited a blaze that lit up the whole baseball world. In June, Martin had demoted Jackson from starting right fielder to the status of a part-time designated hitter, also dropping him from fourth to sixth in the batting order. Both moves upset Jackson, who never suffered in silence. While he stewed, the Yankees played poorly, eventually falling behind the league-leading Red Sox by 15 games. Martin, who wanted to win as much as Jackson did, restored his unhappy slugger to the cleanup spot.

On July 17, the Yankees and Royals were tied, 5–5, in the top of the 10th inning, when Jackson came up with Munson on first and no one out. Managers rarely ask their cleanup hitters to sacrifice, but Martin flashed the bunt sign; the infield crept in; Jackson took a fastball high and inside. Martin then took the bunt sign off, but Jackson bunted at the next pitch anyway, and missed it. Third-base coach Dick

Howser called time and walked down the line to confer with Jackson. "Martin wants you to hit away," he said. "The bunt sign is off."

"I want to bunt," Jackson replied.

"He wants you to swing the bat," Howser repeated emphatically.

Stubbornly ignoring the manager's orders, Jackson bunted at the next two pitches, missing the first and fouling off the second for strike three. The next two batters also failed to bring Munson around, and the Yankees lost the game. Back in the clubhouse, an enraged Martin flung a radio and a bottle against the wall and suspended Jackson indefinitely for "defying me and his teammates."

The incident made the front pages. Jackson flew to his home in Oakland to sit out the suspension, which was reduced to five days. By the time he returned, the volatile Martin was gone, forced to resign after loudly proclaiming to a group of reporters in the Chicago airport that both Jackson and Steinbrenner were habitual liars. As far as Yankees fans were concerned, Martin's firing hardly put an end to the controversy. They had adored Martin since his days as a scrappy second baseman with the Yankees; in any contest between him and Jackson—the outsider—for the fans' support, Martin was going to win in a breeze.

When the new manager, Bob Lemon, reinstated Jackson in right field for a doubleheader against Cleveland, the fans at Yankee Stadium greeted Jackson with boos from the minute he stepped on the field, and they never let up. They cheered when he swung and missed, and they chanted "Bunt, bunt, bunt" at him. As always, the booing inspired Jackson to concentrate more intensely. He had 5 hits that day, including his 15th homer.

Under Lemon's easygoing leadership, the Yankees pulled off one of baseball's greatest comebacks, finishing the season tied for the A.L. East title with Boston, then finishing off the Red Sox on Bucky Dent's home run at Fenway Park in a 1-game playoff. Jackson hit two dingers in the playoff rout of Kansas City, and two more in their 6-game World Series win over the Dodgers.

When the Yankees got off to a slow start in 1979, George Steinbrenner abruptly fired Lemon. Billy Martin returned as manager on June 18, 1979, and made Jackson's life miserable again. In Martin's first game at the helm, the fans stood and cheered him for two solid minutes when he took the lineup card to home plate before the game. Martin apologized to Steinbrenner for calling him a liar, but he never apologized to Jackson. Steinbrenner always said that Jackson was a winner, but he backed Martin whenever the manager took a potshot at the unhappy player.

Jackson missed several weeks with a torn leg muscle, and the idleness further dampened his spirits. "Nobody in New York likes me," he moaned. Even if 50,000 people cheered him when he hit one out, he focused on the few who booed. But he never let up, batting .297 with 29 home runs as the Yankees finished fourth.

When Jackson showed up three days late for spring training in March 1980, Martin was gone again, fired this time for punching a marshmallow salesman in a hotel bar. Dick Howser, the soft-spoken, highly respected coach, replaced him. Howser knew how to stroke a superstar's ego, and Jackson began to feel wanted again. By

August 3, Jackson tied Al Kaline on the all-time home run list with 399, and the vigil began for number 400. The next night, the fans in the right-field seats hung out a sheet with a bull's-eye painted on it, and people crowded the bleachers wearing fielders' gloves. Enjoying the hoopla, Jackson played to the crowd. After one strikeout, he went out to right field, turned to the fans, and shrugged his shoulders in apology.

The wait was over on August 11, when Jackson connected off Britt Burns of the White Sox. Home run number 400 soared into an empty section of the right-field seats. A pack of youngsters scrambled after it, and 10-year-old Cheryl Hanchar got to it first. After the game, she presented the ball to Jackson amid a media circus.

Jackson and the Yankees thrived in that season of tranquillity under the leadership of Dick Howser. Jackson batted .300 for the only time in his career, hit a league-leading 41 homers, and drove in 111 runs. He had turned in an MVP performance; but Kansas City's George Brett batted a phenomenal .390, leading the Royals to the A.L. West crown, and his performance earned him the Most Valuable Player Award. The Yankees won the A.L. East, but the Royals swept the Yankees in the playoff, and Dick Howser lost his job despite winning 103 games during the regular season.

Jackson was distressed enough at losing Howser. Things got worse on December 5, when he watched from the sidelines as Steinbrenner signed free agent outfielder Dave Winfield to a 10-year, $25 million contract, the richest deal in history at that time. Suddenly, right field at Yankee Stadium became crowded.

No longer the top banana, Jackson had to play the 1981 season in the large shadow cast by Winfield, and Steinbrenner made a point of rubbing salt in his wounds. At one point, the owner ordered Jackson to have a medical checkup, suggesting that the player's eyesight might be causing his problems at the plate. Jackson felt humiliated, but he submitted to the examination, which found nothing wrong with him. He finally began to hit in August, but his .237 batting average and 15 home runs were career lows.

A players' strike resulted in the only split

Jackson poses with Dave Winfield, the newest Yankees superstar, before the start of the 1981 season. Winfield's arrival was a bitter blow to Jackson, who suddenly found himself laboring in the shadow of a younger, faster, and more versatile ballplayer.

Yankees owner George Steinbrenner consoles Jackson after the team's 1981 World Series loss to the Los Angeles Dodgers. Both men knew that Jackson had just played his last game in pin-stripes; Steinbrenner later admitted that he made a terrible mistake when he decided not to re-sign Jackson.

season in major league history. The Yankees won the first half in the East, Milwaukee the second. Jackson hit a clutch home run in the Yankees' elimination of the Brewers but batted only four times, without a hit, in New York's sweep of Oakland in the playoffs.

The night they defeated Oakland, the Yankees held a celebratory party. Jackson arrived late with several friends, who sat down at a table that third baseman Graig Nettles and his family had been occupying. When Nettles's party returned to the table and demanded their seats back, angry words were exchanged. Jackson and Nettles wound up in a wild wrestling match, knocking over tables and

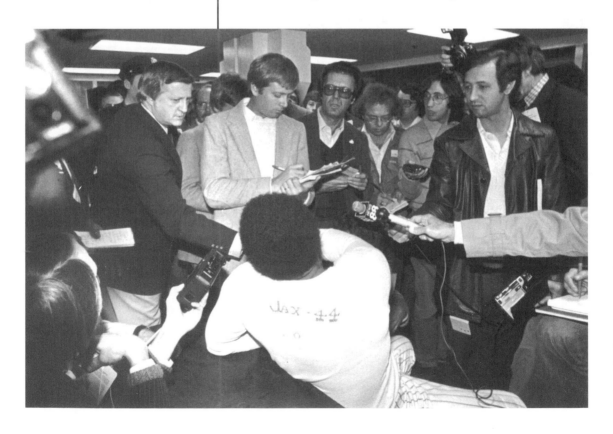

chairs like a pair of saloon brawlers in an old-time western movie. Pitcher Goose Gossage pulled the two men apart and hustled Jackson and his group out of the restaurant. The Nettles family left in tears. Steinbrenner blamed the whole fracas on Jackson and criticized him for bringing outsiders to the team party, calling him the "former number forty-four."

Although Jackson and Nettles made up during the flight back to New York, whatever slim chance there might have been of Jackson staying in New York vanished that night. The morning after the last game of the World Series loss to the Dodgers, he cleaned out his locker at Yankee Stadium, alone and in silence. Jackson's days as a Yankee were over, without a word of appreciation or even a handshake from the owner. For five years, Jackson had been as big a drawing card as any Yankee since Babe Ruth, helping the team set an American League attendance record of 2,627,417 in 1980.

He had come in through the palace gates; he left through the back door.

THE LAST DINGER

Wearing the uniform of the California Angels, Jackson makes contact during a 1982 playoff contest with the Milwaukee Brewers. Proving that there was still plenty of thunder in his familiar black bat, Jackson led the league with 39 homers and sparked his team to a division title.

At the age of 35, Reggie Jackson still had goals to reach, but time was running out. Once again a free agent, he hoped to sign with the Dodgers, but they showed no interest in him. The Orioles and Angels made him offers. Baltimore would be closer to his father in Philadelphia, but Anaheim was closer to his home up the California coast in Carmel. Although he would not be the Angels' highest-paid player, that no longer bothered the more mature Jackson. He signed a four-year contract with the team for $700,000 a year, plus bonuses. Angels manager Gene Mauch called him and said, "All I want is for you to play for me the way you did against me."

Jackson confessed to feeling nervous on April 26, when he made his first visit to New York in a visitor's uniform. He was batting only .173, and with a tough left-hander, Ron Guidry, pitching for New York, Jackson would ordinarily have been benched. But he begged Gene Mauch to let him play, and Mauch decided to take a chance.

When Jackson trotted out to right field in the first inning, the fans gave him a standing ovation. Later, someone ran onto the field and handed him a bouquet of yellow flowers. On his first time at bat, the fans greeted him warmly with the familiar "Reg-GIE! Reg-GIE!" chant. He popped up, but that did not quiet the crowd. They cheered wildly in the fifth when Jackson stroked a single. In the seventh, with the rain coming down, Jackson toweled off his thin-handled black bat, wiped the mist off his glasses, and stepped into the batter's box. He pounced on Guidry's first pitch and treated the fans to the routine they had seen so many times before: still standing at the plate, Jackson dropped his bat, clapped his hands, and admired the flight of the ball—only when it disappeared into the far reaches of the upper deck did he begin his home run trot.

As Jackson slowly circled the bases, Guidry stood on the mound and covered his face with his glove so no one would see him smiling. Catcher Rick Cerone shared Guidry's sentiments. "I felt a little something for him when he was rounding the bases," Cerone admitted. "The guy's dramatic."

Jackson came through with a league-leading 39 home runs in 1982 (upping his lifetime total to 464), and the Angels won the A.L. West. They took the first 2 games of the best-of-5-games playoff in Milwaukee and headed home talking about where to hold the victory party. Jackson eagerly looked forward to one more chance to star on baseball's biggest stage. But the Angels lost 3 straight at home and watched the Series on TV. "We couldn't close the sale," Jackson said. "We were too smug."

Jackson worked hard during the off-season, hoping to reach 500 home runs. But the Angels and Jackson went into a yearlong funk. After winning 93 games in 1982, they lost 92 in 1983.

Jackson was so down that he was even sick of talking about himself. On his first visit to New York, he arrived at Yankee Stadium early to avoid reporters. "Reggie Jackson is a boring subject.... Do people really care?" he complained. "I can't take three steps on the field without every writer and broadcaster in every town following me around asking the same questions." His production at the plate matched his mood: he batted only .194 for the year and could get his home run total only to 478. But he still ran out every ball. And he still brought people to the ballpark. Angels season ticket holders competed for seats in right field just to be out there near him.

The Angels contended for the A.L. West title in 1984 and 1985 and finally won it in 1986. This time they came within 1 out of going to the World Series before blowing a 3-games-to-1 lead and losing to the Red Sox. Jackson continued his climb in the home run standings. On September 17, 1984, at Anaheim Stadium, he hit number 500 off Bud Black of the Royals. In 1985, he passed Ted Williams and Willie McCovey as he reached 530.

A few days after the 1985 season ended, Angels general manager Mike Port called Jackson and told him that the Angels wanted to go with younger players and did not intend to offer him a new contract. But it turned out the Angels were stuck with him; his 27 home runs and 85 RBIs had met the performance requirements that automatically extended his contract for another year at $1 million.

On May 14, 1986, in his 20th big league season, four days shy of his 40th birthday, Jackson boomed his 537th home run off Boston's Roger

At the age of 40, Jackson hustles to break up a double play against the Detroit Tigers in a 1986 contest. Summing up his approach to the game, he once said, "The most important thing to leave is: 'This guy was a champion; this guy was a winner; this guy played hard.'"

Clemens, passing Mickey Mantle for sixth place on the all-time list. He was still emotionally attached to the Yankees, and when he became a free agent again on November 7, 1986, he yearned for a chance to finish his career in New York. But the call never came. Very few calls did. So when the Oakland A's offered him a one-year contract to bow out where he had first become a star, he took it.

Jackson's last circuit of the American League brought his fans out in every city. Finally, Jackson took his familiar black bat to the plate for the last time in Oakland and lined a single. A pinch runner took his place on first base. The A's young slugger, Jose Canseco, was next up. On the first pitch, he tried to bunt. Standing by the dugout, Jackson hollered at him, "Forget that bunt stuff. Stand up there and hit it where they'll need a new ball." For Reggie Jackson, that was always the name of the game.

Throughout his career, Jackson's glorious moments were shadowed by a little black cloud that seemed to hover over him, raining on his parade from time to time as if to remind him that there were stronger forces in the world than Reggie Jackson. Twice his Oakland home burned to the ground, destroying his art and gun collections and his baseball memorabilia. Several of his cars were stolen, and more than once he faced the business end of a gun on the streets of New York.

He could not enjoy a play, a movie, a museum, a meal in a restaurant, or even a walk without being mobbed by autograph seekers. If he refused or asked them to wait until he finished what he was doing, they went away muttering about his attitude.

Jackson was a complex personality—assertive, insecure, and easily hurt. At the age of 21, he had married a fellow student at Arizona State, Jennie Campos, but the marriage lasted only a short time. "I had no idea what marriage was all about," he later admitted. "We all lug our insecurities around like carry-on bags," he said on another occasion. "Mine, I think, came from childhood." Long after he retired, he said that he was still working on getting along with people and understanding them.

Jackson could be a good interviewee or rudely brush off a reporter. He could be charming and friendly, then suddenly go off—on teammates and friends, as well as on strangers—for no apparent reason. Once he tried to get out of paying some accumulated traffic fines by telling a police sergeant, "I'm Reggie Jackson. I don't have to pay." He sat in jail until a bondsman posted bail.

Some players hated him because he would tease and ride them and not know when to stop. But others remember him fondly as a teacher, motivator, counselor, and confidence builder to young players. "There were at least two Reggies," Elrod Hendricks said. "He could be warm and caring, especially with kids. But he did not want people to see that offstage side of him." Hendricks added, "He reached so hard for love he turned people off, not knowing when to stop. He would ride a player until the player got ticked off and told him to get lost; then Reggie would feel hurt and wonder why they didn't like him."

Jackson always picked up his own dirty towels and uniform after a game so that the clubhouse boy did not have to do it. He doted on his nephews and nieces and gave generously to youth organizations in Arizona and New York. But most people saw only the public Reggie Jackson, as magnified by the media.

Perhaps the final assessment of Jackson ought to come from two men with more than half a century of big league managing between them. Gene Mauch, who managed Jackson in California,

Back with the Oakland A's in 1987 for his final season, Jackson tutors rookie slugger Mark McGwire during pregame fielding practice. Though his skills had clearly faded, Jackson was valued by the A's as a motivator and teacher for their talented young players.

said, "It was a pleasure to be his manager.... He had a presence about him that I never saw in any other player, including Ted Williams and Stan Musial. It was more than charisma. It was indefinable. Every black player in the league was in awe of him." Sparky Anderson, who often had the task of trying to beat Jackson's teams, said that Jackson, Dave Winfield, and Pete Rose were the three players he had seen during his career who gave their all on every play of the game.

Many players have a difficult time adjusting to the changes in their lives when they hang up their spikes, and Jackson was no different. In 1988 and 1989, Jackson suffered some business losses and had little success finding a job in baseball. His reputation as an individualist may have prevented people from seeing him as part of a corporate team. But he persevered, and by 1993, Jackson was a vice-president and director of the Upper Deck baseball card company and an adviser to Yankees owner George Steinbrenner, who admitted that letting Jackson go in 1981 had been his biggest mistake.

In January 1993, Jackson was elected to the Hall of Fame with 396 votes out of a possible 423. When nobody else was selected to share the induction platform with him, baseball people thought it was more than fitting to have Jackson in sole possession of the spotlight at Cooperstown. Given the choice of which team cap he wanted on his plaque, he chose the Yankees. "I believe I'm most remembered for what happened in New York," he explained.

On Sunday, August 1, 1993, Jackson fidgeted during the hours leading up to his induction ceremony, talking to some of the 39 Hall of Famers present for the events, worrying that his speech was too long and that he could not get through it without breaking down. He knew that he would be looking out at his father and mother in the front row, as well as his longtime friend and business adviser Gary Walker.

That afternoon, looking out at the crowd that greeted him with the familiar chant of "Reg-GIE! Reg-GIE!" Jackson acknowledged the debt he owed to family and friends and to Jackie Robinson and the other black players who had paved the way for him. He concluded not by praising his own deeds, as some might have expected, but by revealing the more thoughtful and sensitive side of his personality: "I know I wasn't the best.... But it's nice to know when they have roll call, sooner or later, they're going to call my name.... Whether you are the Babe, Stan the Man, Say Hey, or Mr. October, you're just part of a long tradition of baseball.... We're all just a link in a chain."

CHRONOLOGY

1946	Born Reginald Martinez Jackson in Wyncote, Pennsylvania, on May 16
1964	Enrolls at Arizona State University on a football scholarship
1966	Drafted by Kansas City Athletics
1967	Plays most of season in minor leagues at Birmingham, Alabama; hits first major league home run on September 17
1968	Becomes starting right fielder for Oakland A's and finishes season with 29 home runs
1969	Achieves national celebrity with home run hitting during first half of season; finishes with 47 home runs
1973	Wins American League Most Valuable Player Award after hitting 32 home runs and driving in 117 runs; chosen World Series MVP after leading A's to their second consecutive world championship
1974	Leads all players in voting for All-Star team; A's win third straight World Series
1976	Jackson is traded to the Baltimore Orioles; becomes a free agent after the season and signs five-year, $2.9 million contract with the New York Yankees
1977	Hits three home runs in Game 7 of the World Series as the Yankees beat the Los Angeles Dodgers
1980	Hits 400th career home run; bats .300 for first time in his career and leads league with 41 home runs
1982	Signs as free agent with the California Angels; leads league with 39 home runs
1984	Hits 500th career home run
1986	Signs one-year contract with Oakland A's
1987	Retires with 563 career home runs, sixth-highest total in baseball history
1993	Inducted into National Baseball Hall of Fame

REGINALD MARTINEZ JACKSON
"MR. OCTOBER"

KANSAS CITY, A.L., 1967
OAKLAND, A.L., 1968-1975, 1987
BALTIMORE, A.L., 1976
NEW YORK, A.L., 1977-1981
CALIFORNIA, A.L., 1982-1986

EXCITING PERFORMER WHO PLAYED FOR 11 DIVISION WINNERS AND
FOUND SPECIAL SUCCESS IN WORLD SERIES SPOTLIGHT WITH 10 HOME
RUNS, 24 RBI'S AND .357 BATTING AVERAGE IN 27 GAMES. IN 1977
SERIES, HIT RECORD 5 HOMERS, 4 OF THEM CONSECUTIVE, INCLUDING
3 IN ONE GAME ON 3 FIRST PITCHES OFF 3 DIFFERENT HURLERS.
MAMMOTH CLOUT MARKED 1971 ALL STAR GAME. 563 HOMERS RANK
6TH ON ALL-TIME LIST. A.L. MVP, 1973.

MAJOR LEAGUE STATISTICS

KANSAS CITY ATHLETICS, OAKLAND A'S, BALTIMORE ORIOLES, NEW YORK YANKEES, CALIFORNIA ANGELS

YEAR	TEAM	G	AB	R	H	2B	3B	HR	RBI	BA	SB
1967	KC A	35	118	13	21	4	4	1	6	.178	1
1968	OAK A	154	553	82	138	13	6	29	74	.250	14
1969		152	549	123	151	36	3	47	118	.275	13
1970		149	426	57	101	21	2	23	66	.237	26
1971		150	567	87	157	29	3	32	80	.277	16
1972		135	499	72	132	25	2	25	75	.265	9
1973		151	539	99	158	28	2	32	117	.293	22
1974		148	506	90	146	25	1	29	93	.289	25
1975		157	593	91	150	39	3	36	104	.253	17
1976	BAL A	134	498	84	138	27	2	27	91	.277	28
1977	NY A	146	525	93	150	39	2	32	110	.286	17
1978		139	511	82	140	13	5	27	97	.274	14
1979		131	465	78	138	24	2	29	89	.297	9
1980		143	514	94	154	22	4	41	111	.300	1
1981		94	334	33	79	17	1	15	54	.237	0
1982	CAL A	153	530	92	146	17	1	39	101	.275	4
1983		116	397	43	77	14	1	14	49	.194	0
1984		143	525	67	117	17	2	25	81	.223	8
1985		143	460	64	116	27	0	27	85	.252	1
1986		132	419	65	101	12	2	18	58	.241	1
1987	OAK A	115	336	42	74	14	1	15	43	.220	2
Totals		2820	9864	1551	2584	463	49	563	1702	.262	228

World Series

5 years		27	98	21	35	7	1	10	24	.357	1

FURTHER READING

Angeli, Michael. "The Gall of Fame." *Sports Illustrated,* August 2, 1993.

Burchard, Marshall. *Sports Hero, Reggie Jackson.* New York: Putnam, 1975.

Gutman, Bill. *Picture Life of Reggie Jackson.* New York: Franklin Watts, 1978.

Hahn, James, and Lynn Hahn. *Reggie Jackson: Slugger Supreme.* St. Paul, MN: EMC, 1979.

Libby, Bill. *Reggie: A Season with a Superstar.* Chiacgo: Playboy Press, 1975.

———. *The Reggie Jackson Story.* New York: Lothrop, Lee & Shepard, 1979.

Lupica, Mike. *Reggie: The Autobiography.* New York: Villard Books, 1984.

INDEX

aron, Hank, 18
i, Muhammad, 18
iderson, Sparky, 56
rizona State University (ASU), 19, 21, 23, 53
altimore Orioles, 23, 30, 31, 36, 39, 49
ando, Sal, 22
aseball Hall of Fame, 11, 56
auer, Hank, 23, 28
rett, George, 13, 44
alifornia Angels, 49, 50, 51
anseco, Jose, 53
armel, California, 49
hambliss, Chris, 10, 39
ncinnati Reds, 32, 36
ent, Bucky, 43
nley, Charles, 25, 29, 30, 31, 35, 36
ster, Gene, 19
bson, Bob, 18
bson, Josh, 16
ossage, Goose, 47
uidry, Ron, 49, 50
ealy, Fran, 37, 38
endricks, Elrod, 30, 33, 54
owser, Dick, 41, 42, 43
ckson, Beverly (sister), 15, 16
ckson, Clara (mother), 15, 16, 22, 57
ckson, Clarence (half brother), 15, 16
ckson, Dolores (half sister), 15, 16
ckson, James (brother), 15, 16
ckson, Jennie Campos (wife), 53
ckson, Martinez (father), 15, 16, 17, 19, 24, 49, 57
ckson, Reggie
  All–Star Games, 12, 35
  A.L. playoff appearances, 31, 35, 39, 43, 44, 46, 50, 51
  as Baltimore Oriole, 36
  big league debut, 25

birth, 15
as California Angel, 49 –52
childhood, 15 –19
college years, 19 –24
divorce, 53
football career, 12, 17, 19, 21, 23, 24
home run, 500th, 51
home run, 400th, 44
home runs in 1977 World Series, 9 –12, 39
as free agent, 12, 35, 52
Hall of Fame induction, 56 –57
as Kansas City Athletic, 24, 25
marriage, 53
minor league career, 25
MVP Award, 32, 35
as New York Yankee, 9 –12, 36, 49
as Oakland A, 27–35
pro contract, signs, 24 –25
and racism, 15, 16, 23
retirement from baseball, 53, 56
as vice–president of Upper Deck, 56
World Series appearances, 9 –12, 31, 32, 35, 39, 43, 47
Jackson, Tina (sister), 15, 16
Kaline, Al, 44
Kansas City Athletics, 17, 24, 25, 27. See also Oakland A's
Kansas City Royals, 13, 33, 39, 41, 43, 44, 51
King, Martin Luther, Jr., 19
Kush, Frank, 21, 24
Lemon, Bob, 41, 42, 43
Los Angeles Dodgers, 9, 10, 11, 12, 35, 39, 43, 47, 49
McCovey, Willie, 51
Mantle, Mickey, 22, 28, 52
Maris, Roger, 27, 28
Martin, Billy, 38, 39, 41, 43
Mauch, Gene, 49, 54

Mays, Willie, 18, 57
Monday, Rick, 22, 24
Munson, Thurman, 36, 37, 39, 41, 42
Musial, Stan, 56, 57
Negro leagues, 16
Nettles, Graig, 46, 47
New York City, 9, 36, 37, 39, 43, 47, 49, 51, 54, 56
New York Mets, 32
New York Yankees, 9, 10, 36, 37, 38, 39, 41, 42, 43, 44, 45, 46, 47, 49, 52, 56
Oakland, California, 27, 42, 53
Oakland A's, 27, 31, 32, 35, 36, 46, 52, 53. See also Kansas City Athletics
Paige, Satchel, 16
Palmer, Jim, 12
Randolph, Willie, 10, 12
Robinson, Frank, 12, 29, 30
Robinson, Jackie, 18, 57
Rose, Pete, 56
Ruth, Babe, 11, 27, 47, 57
Steinbrenner, George, 38, 41, 42, 43, 44, 45, 47, 56
Upper Deck baseball card company, 56
Walker, Gary, 57
Williams, Dick, 29
Williams, Ted, 51, 56
Winfield, Dave, 44, 45, 56
Winkles, Bobby, 22, 24
Winter League, 30
World Series
  1972, 31, 32
  1973, 31, 32
  1974, 31, 35
  1977, 9 –12, 39
  1978, 43
  1981, 47
Wyncote, Pennsylvania, 15, 19
Yankee Stadium, 9, 42, 45, 47, 51

NORMAN L. MACHT was a minor league general manager with the Milwaukee Braves and Baltimore Orioles organizations and has been a stockbroker and college professor. His work has appeared in *The BallPlayers, The Sporting News, Baseball Digest, USA Today Baseball Weekly,* and *Sports Heritage,* and he is the coauthor with Dick Bartell of *Rowdy Richard* and with Rex Barney of *THANK Youuu for Fifty Years of Baseball.* Norman Macht lives in Baltimore, Maryland.

JIM MURRAY, veteran sports columnist of the *Los Angeles Times,* is one of America's most acclaimed writers. He has been named "America's Best Sportswriter" by the National Association of Sportscasters and Sportswriters 14 times, was awarded the Red Smith Award, and was twice winner of the National Headliner Award. In addition, he was awarded the J. G. Taylor Spink Award in 1987 for "meritorious contributions to baseball writing." With this award came his 1988 induction into the National Baseball Hall of Fame in Cooperstown, New York. In 1990, Jim Murray was awarded the Pulitzer Prize for Commentary.

EARL WEAVER is the winningest manager in the Baltimore Orioles' history by a wide margin. He compiled 1,480 victories in his 17 years at the helm. After managing eight different minor league teams, he was given the chance to lead the Orioles in 1968. Under his leadership the Orioles finished lower than second place in the American League East only four times in 17 years. One of only 12 managers in big league history to have managed in four or more World Series, Earl was named Manager of the Year in 1979. The popular Weaver had his number 5 retired in 1982, joining Brooks Robinson, Frank Robinson, and Jim Palmer, whose numbers were retired previously. Earl Weaver continues his association with the professional baseball scene by writing, broadcasting, and coaching.